LIFE
without
LIMITS

Achieve the Life You Want
in Just Minutes
a Day

D1595520

M K JACKSON

Copyright 2021 © M K Jackson

ISBN: 978-1-955622-99-8

Published by

Fideli Publishing
119 W Morgan St
Martinsville, IN 46151

www.FideliPublishing.com

To book the author for events or to ask questions about this book, please email the author at:

marsha@mkjbooks.com

visit the author's website:

LifeWithoutLimitsBook.com

Foreword

Self Motivation...with it, nothing else really matters.
Without it, nothing else works.

Most people are resigned to believe that "they are just the way they are" and there isn't really anything they can do about it. They tend to live quiet lives of desperation. Some people have that spark of curiosity and wonder. "I wonder where I could go. I wonder what I could do. I wonder who I could be." These are all profound questions that can lead to the journey of discovering all we can be. People that live this journey end up in an entirely different place in life but more importantly walk an amazing path of adventure, growth, friendship, contribution, love and self satisfaction.

Marsha's 31 exercises are a brilliant way to launch yourself into an orbit of a new you. Not a you absent of your core values but a you amplified, celebrated and exponential. Most people will never purchase this book. Most people that do will never actually pick it up and start reading it. Most people that do will not actually do the exercises. That is the nature of us.

What is your nature? Do you dabble? Do you try and get distracted? Do you start and rarely finish? Or do you have the extraordinary nature that has you lean in to every opportunity for adventure and education?

You have in your hands a gift…a gift of Marsha Jackson's own inquiry into her life well lived. What will you do with it? What is your life worth? What are your dreams worth?

We are about to find out. Read on. Dive in. You will love the water.

Richard Bliss Brooke

Author, *Mach 2, The Art of Vision and Self Motivation*

31 Days to a New You

This book offers 31 principles and corresponding daily meditations to help you transform yourself and your relationships. If you take one day at a time and practice the activities I suggest each day, then you will see results.

Can you do one simple exercise a day? Now, I'm not talking about physical exercise (though that may be a lot easier after we get through the next 31 days). I'm talking about searching yourself for answers and reprogramming your mind. Currently, your mind is like a computer that isn't working properly. I'm going to help you "fix" your mind to empower you to achieve what you want to achieve.

To begin to think differently, you need to reprogram your **mind** daily. When you **think** differently, you begin to **act** differently, and then your outcomes can be **different**.

Are you willing to **invest** in yourself for the next 31 days to **change things forever**? I believe in you and at the end of these 31 days, you will, too. You have the capabilities within your grasp to **change your life forever!**

Remember, the definition of insanity is doing the same thing over and over again and expecting to achieve different results. It's time to break out and do something different.

Get ready ... Get set...*GO!*

Table of Contents

USE THE 4 Rs TO CREATE THE

READ the subject matter for the day.

REFLECT on what you have just read and how it applies to you.

RESET your mind to begin the new thought processes.

REDO and make the necessary changes to complete the action steps.

As you direct yourself through this four-step process each day, you will find that these simple steps will help you change where you are and direct you toward a brighter future.

ENJOY THE NEW YOU!

Author's Note

I have used all the principles I recommend in this book and continue to use them every day of my life. Reprogramming my mind to think this way both changed the trajectory of my life and positively affected the people in my sphere of influence. I hope you will allow these principles to do the same for you.

If you need more than one day to work through a section, then definitely take the time. It's worth the extra effort to make sure the changes you want to make become a part of your daily life.

"If you can dream it,
you can do it."

~ WALT DISNEY

Motivation

W e begin with this one because if you are going to make a transformation within the next 31 days, you will need some motivation along the way.

What does it mean to be motivated? Motivation is the process that initiates, guides, and maintains goal-oriented behaviors. It causes you to act, whether it is getting a glass of water to quench thirst or reading a book to gain knowledge.

Motivation involves the biological, emotional, social, and cognitive forces that activate behavior. In everyday usage, the word "motivation" is frequently used to describe why a person does something. It is the driving force behind human actions.

Motivation doesn't just refer to the factors that activate behaviors, it also involves the factors that direct and maintain these goal-directed actions (though such motives are rarely directly observable). As a result, we often have to infer the reasons why people do the things that they do based on observable behaviors.

Definition from Very Well Mind (https://www.verywellmind. com/what-is-motivation-2795378).

I don't believe that motivation is something you can just muster up instantly. Motivation to do something always has an underlying reason. As we begin this journey, I want you to take a little time each day to not only think about, but to meditate on the thought I leave with you and begin to let your brain process the thoughts that go through your mind.

Remember, you are a computer that needs to be reprogrammed. Be deliberate in your thoughts and focus for the next 31 days. When I talk about meditating, I mean focused thought. Taking the time, even if it is five minutes a couple times a day, to focus your thoughts on the meditation each day and working through your thoughts.

Your brain is fascinating, really! You can actually trick your brain into believing something that is not yet true, but will eventually become true if you will begin to see yourself already there.

You might say that sounds crazy. Well, it just might, but the method works. If you don't believe me, let's do a quick exercise.

Find a spot with an elevated ledge or step that will allow you to balance with your toes and the front part of your feet resting on the edge, and the remaining two-thirds of your feet above ground level. The ledge should be about six inches high to keep your feet from touching the ground.

Close your eyes and imagine yourself teetering on the ledge of a tall building, almost falling off. If you take enough time to fully imagine this scene and focus your attention on the action of the falling, your brain will believe it is a real experience and prepare you for the fall. You may even find your heart rate speeding up.

Now that you understand how you might visualize an outcome, think about what you might imagine in a positive way.

MEDITATION

Focus on one aspect in your life that you want to change by the end of these 31 days. Here are some examples of behaviors and mindsets people often want to change:

- **Reacting in a more positive way**
- **Being more controlled when becoming angry**
- **Looking at my day filled with hope, etc.**

Tomorrow, we will build onto this thought. For today, meditate and visualize the aspect you want to change as if it were already true.

"*A man of personality
can formulate ideals,
but only a man of character
can achieve them.*"

~ HERBERT READ

Character

You may not like who you are, or you may want to change just some of your character traits, or you may wish to acquire new traits. I want you to pick out three character qualities you admire in others that you would like to have for yourself. What do I mean by this?

Often we go through life and notice great qualities in others like boldness, certainty, communication, compassion, and fearlessness. The list goes on and on. We see these admirable character traits in others and think that we cannot have them for ourselves.

Remember what we talked about yesterday? You can reprogram your mind like a computer. Yes, we were all born with specific personality traits, but we also have the ability to become more than who we are.

Are you willing to do what each day requires to become that which you have wanted to be for so long? What have you got to lose?

I have created a list of positive qualities to spark your thinking about whom you want to be, but I bet you can think of many more qualities you admire. Select three qualities that you would like to be known for from my list or your own list. Next, think about what these qualities might look like in your life:

- **How would you act differently on a daily basis?**

- **How would others react to you?**

- **How would this quality propel you forward in your relationships and work place?**

"Every person has a different view
of another person's image.
That's all perception.
The character of a man, the integrity,
that's who you are."

~ STEVE ALFORD

LIST OF POSITIVE QUALITIES

Accomplishment	Creativity	Moderation
Adaptability	Decisive	Openness
Assertiveness	Dependable	Optimism
Ambition	Discipline	Passion
Attentive	Drive	Patience
Achievement	Endurance	Peace
Balance	Excellence	Persistence
Boldness	Fearless	Poise
Bravery	Focus	Restraint
Calm	Generosity	Risk
Capable	Giving	Security
Certainty	Gratitude	Self-reliance
Clear	Honesty	Selfless
Commitment	Hope	Sensitivity
Communication	Imagination	Skillful
Compassion	Inspiring	Spontaneous
Confidence	Kindness	Strength
Consistency	Leadership	Thankful
Control	Love	Thoughtful
Courage	Loyalty	Vision

MEDITATION

I want you to see yourself exhibiting the three qualities you selected in your life. What do these qualities look like in your daily behaviors? What do you need to do in order to embody that quality?

EXAMPLE

I chose being more dependable as one of my qualities. First, I see myself fulfilling everything I say I will do. I hear people call me a dependable person. Secondly, I identify what I need to do to make myself more dependable:

- Don't bite off more than I can chew (or do).
- Keep track of what I say I will do.
- When a commitment I made is an inconvenience or I am financially burdened by doing what I said I would, I will do it anyway, and learn from the experience.

Purpose

Do you ever wonder why you are here? Does life seem so difficult and every day a chore? Do you ask yourself, Why can't I see what I am destined for now?

I think we all have felt that way at one time or another and there are so many books on this subject. Let me present you with a thought … Life is a journey with multiple destinations!

You are here for not just A Purpose, but for many purposes that will be discovered in your life while on your personal journey. Enjoy the journey as you go through this life and learn from all the mistakes you make. Many people don't realize until later in life that you cannot have success without failure. Look at successful people like Babe Ruth and Thomas Edison. For many years Babe Ruth not only had the most home runs, but he also had many strikeouts, but what is he remembered for? He is remembered for his home runs. Thomas Edison said that he didn't fail 100 times; he found 100 ways the light bulb didn't work.

Purpose could be defined as the reason why something is done or created, or why something exists.

You exist not only for yourself, but also for everyone your life touches and beyond. The questions I ask myself are: What will be said and remembered of me when I die? What kind of life do I have and what kind of life do I want to have? Who has my voice impacted?

You can have meaningful purpose every single day of your life. How you might ask? This is a multi-faceted topic that I will be touching upon throughout these 31 days. You have different areas of your life that need to be changed to have the effect upon your world around you that you were created for. We will work through these different areas in the coming days.

One day at a time and you will be victorious.

I BELIEVE IN YOU!

If I can overcome fear, rejection, depression, and failures,

YOU CAN, TOO.

Can you eat an elephant?

YES. ONE BITE AT A TIME.

MEDITATION

WHAT WILL YOU BE REMEMBERED FOR?

When people look at your life, what do you think they see? Whose lives have been uplifted and improved because of you?

WHAT ON EARTH ARE YOU HERE FOR?

Look at your desires and talents, because these play an important part in your purpose. One book that can help you answer some of these questions and give you some guidance is *The Purpose Driven Life* by Rick Warren.

Your purpose will be more than one thing. You will find that your purposes in life all seem to have a common thread. As you think about what you have done in the past, what you are doing now, and what you want to do in the future, focus on what they all seem to have in common. Be aware that some of your purposes or callings will start and come to an end, while some will continue and intertwine with new ones.

"I think anything is possible
if you have the mindset
and the will
and desire to do it
and put the time in."

~ ROGER CLEMENS

Desire

Have you ever wanted something so badly that it was all you could think about? Desire is defined as a strong feeling of wanting to have something or wishing for something to happen.

How can you make a desire a reality? One of the most essential ways to move towards your desires is to define them in a way that makes the goals clear. If you say that you have a desire to work with animals because you love animals, that statement is too vague to give you any kind of direction. Would you go into a restaurant and say that you would like some food? No, you would not. Most people would be very specific as to what kind of salad dressing and toppings with their salad as well as what kind of entrée and how they would like it prepared.

Too many times in life we dream and desire but don't add specific details because we really don't think our desires will become reality. If we don't detail what we want and try to attain our goals, then we don't feel disappointed because we really never tried.

Does this sound familiar?

Here are some questions to ask yourself when you are defining your desires. As an example, we will use the desire to work with animals.

- Where would you like to see yourself working in that field?
- What aspect of working with animals would you enjoy? For example, caring and feeding, training, medical care, and domestic or exotic animals.

Begin to explore what is involved in what you desire to do and the many facets that could go along with it. As you explore, when you come across an aspect that you could not see yourself doing, discard that part. When you see aspects that you really like, explore those aspects further.

Research others who are doing what you desire and study them. If possible, seek them out and talk with them. Once you have a definite direction as to your desire and where you would like to see yourself, no matter how lofty the goal, identify what you need to do first to follow that path. Begin taking small steps everyday to accomplish your desired goal. Consistency is the key to success!

Every great desire and dream starts with a Vision, which we will discuss tomorrow, and the questions you need to ask yourself. Read about how Disney was started. His story will inspire you:

https://www.history.com/this-day-in-history/
walt-disney-company-founded

MEDITATION

Ask yourself these questions and answer them honestly:

- **What would bring me great joy everyday?**

- **Where would I like to see myself?**

- **Why do I desire this?**

"Human behavior flows
from three main sources:
desire, emotion, and knowledge."

~ PLATO

"*A dream is your creative vision for your life in the future.*
You must break out of your current comfort zone and become comfortable with the unfamiliar and the unknown."

~ DENIS WAITLEY

Vision

What you desire is only a dream until you begin to believe it and see yourself there. Your vision will help you lay out what you need to do to get you what you desire. Your vision also affirms you already are what you desire! It is in the first-person present tense. Language is the architect of belief.

We will need to change your thought pattern. All your visions and self-talk must align.

Visions are what you imagine your life to be and self-talk is what you are telling yourself every day. If you see yourself living in a $100,000 house in the future, but tell yourself you can't afford this or that on a daily basis then your vision and self-talk are not aligning and your brain knows it.

The stories we tell ourselves are the visions we buy. The visions we buy determine where and how we fly. Your vision will empower your desire and your dreams and speak to your subconscious mind on a daily basis to do and go forward with what is necessary to be where you want to be. You need to envision yourself as already there.

Vision is storytelling to yourself. Give yourself permission to see your story as you would like it to be as if it already was. Make word pictures of what you do want with no negative wording or thoughts. If you were to make a movie of your life and what you are dreaming of, how would that look? I want you to make it so vivid that it seems real to you. I want you to replay this in your mind over and over again until you believe it. The subconscious mind is powerful.

"The one thing that you have that

nobody else has is you.

Your voice, your mind, your story,

your vision.

So write and draw and build and play and

dance and live as only you can."

NEIL GAIMAN

MEDITATION

Replay over and over a movie about you — the plot of this movie is where you want to be and what you want to be doing.

Watch your words. Every time you catch yourself speaking or thinking negatively, STOP and replace the negativity with positive words and thoughts.

Tomorrow we will get into more detail on this method.

"Excellence comes from how one undertakes to do something. It all begins with the thought process — which is creative and exalted to produce something out of the ordinary."

~ PANKAJ PATEL

Thought Processes

Yesterday we started to get into how you think and what you tell yourself. I want you to ask yourself this question: Would you allow someone to talk to your kids the way you talk to yourself?

We all are so hard on ourselves, but how can we stop this endless cycle? Remember the computer we talked about? We need to continue to reprogram our mind. It takes about three weeks to form a new habit.

First step to reprogramming your mind is recognizing what needs to be changed. Take a few minutes to look at yourself and determine what it is you need to change that will not only make your life better but the lives of everyone around you. If you are unsure of what you think of yourself at this moment, think about what you say to yourself when you feel insecure or afraid of something.

If it is to be, it is up to me.

Now that you have recognized what needs to be changed, let's begin by changing it one thought and action at a time. When a negative thought comes into your mind, **STOP** and say to yourself, *CANCEL-CANCEL*. Then, replace the negative thought with a positive one.

Here's an example. I am at the grocery store and I suddenly realize I have forgotten my grocery list. I say to myself, you idiot, I can't believe you forgot your list. You are never going to remember all that was on that list.

I catch myself thinking about myself negatively and immediately say, CANCEL-CANCEL. I will remember what is on that list and as I walk through the store it will come to me. I have a mind as sharp as a tack.

As you begin to recognize and change these thought patterns, you will begin to automatically think more positive. You will notice that as you continue to practice this, you will indeed become a more positive person.

MEDITATION

Focus on the positive and what you have done right.

If you recognize negative thoughts are slipping in, conscientiously replace them with positive ones.

If you need reminders, write these meditations and positive affirmations on note cards or sticky notes and post them throughout your home.

"Shutting off the thought process
is not rejuvenating;
the mind is like a car battery —
it recharges by running."

~ BILL WATTERSON

"Successful people maintain a positive focus in life no matter what is going on around them."

~ JACK CANFIELD

DAY 7

Focus

Focus brings clarity and definition to your vision. What are you focused on? Do you have clarity of what is important to you, what you are working toward, and do you have a goal in mind (physically, financially, spiritually, emotionally, and relationally)? If you do not have focus, you can end up going in the direction of whatever and whoever cries the loudest.

If you do not have clarity in these areas, it will make it very difficult for you to make decisions and move forward. Let's break this down into smaller pieces so we can grasp it.

As we stated in one of the previous days, vision is where you want to be and where you begin to envision yourself. The next step is to begin to break that down and focus on the steps to be taken over the next few months and years (however lofty the vision and the reasonable amount of time to accomplish that vision).

If you don't know where you want to be in the months and years broken down, then I suggest taking a little time and preparing a plan of what that would look like. If you don't know where you want to go, then how in the world are you going to get there?

A lack of focus is like getting in a car and saying you are going somewhere but you do not know your destination. Would anyone in their right mind do that? If you do not have clear direction, then obviously you will not be going anywhere. You may end up somewhere in twenty or thirty years and ask yourself, how did I get here?

Intentionality is moving in a direction of choice with thought out steps and direction.

MEDITATION

Where do you want to be:

- Three months from now?
- In six months?
- In a year?

Get a clear picture of this in all aspects of your life. Look forward to what you want in five years, ten years, and so forth. Once you have a goal in mind and you are clear and focused on what and where you want to be, begin to break down your destination into daily and weekly tasks. Look at these as stepping-stones to get you closer to the object that you are focused on. No goal is too lofty. Dream big.

Let me give you an example of what this process would look like using what we have learned so far.

Goal and focus: I would like to be 15 pounds lighter three months from now.

We also need to answer the following questions before moving forward: Why do I want to lose weight? What is my motivation?

Thought process and vision: I will envision myself at the lower weight and see myself looking good in the clothes I haven't been able to wear. I will also think about how I will feel about myself at this new weight. I will say to myself, "I feel great and I look great after losing those extra pounds."

Steps to get there: Set a weekly goal. For example, I will cut my calorie intake and exercise more. I will learn what my calorie intake needs to be in order to lose the weight. (Google is your friend here.) My daily goal is to keep my caloric intake at or below the number needed. I will also set a goal for how many times a week I will exercise. Finally, I will speak positive affirmations to myself daily, and when a negative thoughts enter my mind, I will replace them with positive ones.

Consistency is the key to success. More on this after we talk about goals.

*"Live life to the fullest,
and focus on the positive."*

~ MATT CAMERON

Goals

We all have some sort of goals. They could vary from weight, career, eating healthier, exercising, and so forth. Goals are important because they give you something to shoot for. It has been said that if you have nothing to shoot for, you won't hit it.

Let me ask you a few questions:

- Would you buy a house without a closing date?

- Would you go into a restaurant and tell the staff that you just want some food, or would you be specific about what you actually want?

Think about that. Just as we are specific about other areas in our lives, we need to be specific when we are setting goals. Your mind has a way of looking for solutions subconsciously when you set a goal before you and are specific about it.

Goals need to be clear.

Make your goals with the acronym SMART in mind. In this instance, SMART stands for the following:

Specific — Goal or task completed when accomplished

Motivating — Meaningful and brings forth an energy

Attainable — Reasonable in the time period you allot

Relevant — Aligned with your goals

Trackable — Measurable

Set clear goals and then what you need to do or action steps needed to acquire those goals. What are you going to do on a daily basis to get you there? What do you need to accomplish it? When are you going to reach that goal?

You need to be specific when making your goals and you need to write them down.

"I don't focus on what I'm up against. I focus on my goals and I try to ignore the rest."

~ VENUS WILLIAMS

MEDITATION

Write down one goal you would like to accomplish by the end of 30 days.

Now, what do you need to do on a daily basis to accomplish that goal?

Here's an example:

Goal: I would like to lose ten pounds.

Steps I need to take:

- I will not eat after 7 p.m. each night

- I will exercise at least three times a week — Monday, Wednesday, and Friday — and I will do it as soon as I get up.

- I will take the dog for at least one walk each day.

- I will weigh myself weekly and keep track of my progress.

- I will put a smiley face on each day I am successful.

- After 30 days, when I have reached my goal to lose ten pounds, I will reward myself with something I enjoy.

"Success isn't always about greatness.

It's about consistency.
Consistent hard work
leads to success.
Greatness will come."

~ DWAYNE JOHNSON

Consistency

I f you will consistently take positive steps every day, no matter how small or insignificant they may seem, you will see positive results.

I cannot stress this enough. Consistency is the conformity of the application of something. Consistency requires doing it again and again and again.

I talked about weight loss yesterday. If I am serious about the weight loss, I need to consistently make small choices every day to make progress toward that goal. Instead of having that second helping at dinner time, I opt to pass on it. Instead of having that dessert or drink after dinner, I go for a fifteen- to twenty-minute walk. Over time, these small changes will make a huge difference. This technique works with more than just weight loss.

MEDITATION

Name one thing you can change today and be consistent about doing every day from this point forward?

Now make a list of other things you would like to change and what you can do on a daily basis to make that change happen. Only implement one of the items on your list at a time. Once the change has become habit, move on to the next thing on your list.

"It's not all about talent.
It's about dependability,
consistency, and being able to improve.
If you work hard and you're coachable,
and you understand what you need to do,
you can improve."

~ BILL BELICHICK

Priorities

Yesterday we talked about consistency, which is going to have a play on today's activity. Notice that each day will set you up for greater **success** as you continue on your 31-day journey to a BETTER YOU.

What do you value most? If I looked through your bank records and your daily schedule, I could tell you what your top priorities are just by seeing where you allocate your money and spend your time. The interesting thing is that we get caught up in the hubbub of life and many times veer from our priorities.

Today I want you to identify your top three priorities, set them smack dab in front of you and become intentional about putting your money and time where your mouth is.

Understand that clarifying these three top priorities just means these come first; you can have many other things in your life. Think of it like filling a jar. The three top priorities will be three large rocks. After these are placed in the jar, you still have space to add smaller pebbles that represent other little things that occupy your life. You also can add sand, which represents the things in your life that grate you the wrong way and that are not so pleasant.

A few examples of what your priorities might be:

- Health
- Business
- Wealth
- God
- Family
- Travel

Once you have written down your three top priorities in life, I want you to list the top three goals for each priority that you want to accomplish over the next year. Then, mark the number-one goal for each priority. Strive, on a daily basis, to contribute to these goals for each priority in your life.

For example, one of my priorities is health. My three goals are: lose fifteen pounds, achieve better cardiovascular shape so I can run three miles without effort, and feel comfortable in whatever I wear (size 8).

The number-one goal I will focus on connected to this priority is to run three miles without effort. I can achieve this goal by walking/running at least three times a week, starting with one mile and increasing to two miles, etc. I will keep track of when I exercise on my calendar.

MEDITATION

Write down something that is extremely important to you — something you cannot live without.

Next, write down what you would like to improve over the next year.

Think about why these things are priorities for you.

Note, your priorities can change, and that's okay.

"Our life is the sum total
of all the decisions we make every day,
and those decisions are determined
by our priorities."

~ MYLES MUNROE

*"Take accountability...
Blame is the water in which many
dreams and
relationships drown."*

~ STEVE MARABOLI

Accountability

The definition of accountability is taking or being assigned responsibility for something that you have done or something you are supposed to do.

An example of accountability is when an employee admits an error she made on a project. (Source: www.yourdictionary.com/accountability)

What other meanings come to mind?

- Responsible

- Obligation

- True to your word

- Answer to someone

As you progress through these daily activities, you will find that if you can bring in an accountability partner (someone you report to or someone who is participating with you), your success will be greater.

We all need encouragement sometimes, and when we have someone that will hold us responsible to complete the daily activities we've assigned ourselves,we will be more likely to follow through.

"Accountability breeds

response-ability."

~ STEPHEN COVEY

MEDITATION

I want you to choose someone that you can be accountable to. Ask them if they could do the following for you:

- Check in on you daily and ask, "Did you accomplish your daily activity?"

- Encourage you if you falter

- Participate with you in what you're trying to accomplish.

"I have learned over the years that when one's mind
is made up, this diminishes fear; knowing what must be done does away with fear."

~ ROSA PARKS

Fear

Fear is our natural response to protect ourselves, but problems arise when we become so afraid that fear debilitates us and we are unable to progress forward in life.

We have to learn to overcome fear and find the courage to move forward when we know we are not in danger. Courage is not the absence of fear, but going forward and acting in spite of our fears.

Let's use anxiety as an example. Anxiety comes in many forms and has different effects. Whenever I experience anxiety, I get overwhelmed and I just want to shut down. When this occurs, I have to stop what I am doing and take a minute to think about why I am feeling this way. I am recognizing the impact of what is happening. I now begin to speak to my subconscious mind and say to myself, you have no reason to be overwhelmed, just complete one task at a time and in no time, it will be completed. I usually get this overwhelmed feeling when I am doing a big project, be it on the house or in our business.

Two other methods of managing anxiety:

- If I am working on a big project, I will outline it step-by-step and make a list of what I need to do in order to complete it. I can always add to the list if necessary.

- Practice Mel Robbins' five-second rule: when you are feeling anxious or in any way that is not healthy or have bad thoughts, recognize it, and then countdown 5, 4, 3, 2, 1. Then speak to your subconscious and replace the negative thoughts and feelings with positive ones of how you want to feel and think.

I highly recommend reading Mel Robbins' book, *The 5 Second Rule: Transform your Life, Work, and Confidence with Everyday Courage.* The applications in this book are amazing and life changing. She transformed her whole life.

MEDITATION

DO SOMETHING THAT SCARES YOU EVERY DAY!

You might be wondering, "Why is she asking me to do something scary?"

The reason I'm asking you to do this is so that you begin to stretch yourself and do things you normally would not do.

Remember, a rubber band is not useful unless it stretches.

"So then learn to conquer your fear. This is the only art we have to master nowadays: to look at things without fear, and to fearlessly do right."

~ FRIEDRICH DURRENMATT

Inaction breeds doubt and fear.
"Action breeds
confidence and courage.
If you want to conquer fear,
do not sit home and
think about it.
Go out and get busy."

~ DALE CARNEGIE

Courage

We are going to build upon what we talked about yesterday so you can get stronger in this area. Courage is not the absence of fear; but it is in the doing in spite of your fears. Do the thing and you will have the power!

YOU CAN AND YOU WILL!

I remember when we went to Honduras and went snorkeling out in the ocean. It was absolutely beautiful. As we began to venture out farther and farther, I could not see the bottom anymore and began to have anxiety. I felt like I couldn't breathe when I put my head in the water to look around. I stopped thinking bad thoughts about not being able to breathe and told myself, I am all right, I am with a group, and I am safe. All I have to do to breathe is lift my head.

I was not going to let my anxiety ruin this once-in-a-lifetime chance to explore the beauty of the ocean. As I kept thinking these positive thoughts, the anxiety began to leave me.

Was I afraid? Yes!

Did I let my fears overtake me? No! I had courage in spite of my fears.

"I learned that courage
was not the absence of fear,
but the triumph over it.
The brave man is not
he who does not feel afraid,
but he who conquers that fear."

~ NELSON MANDELA

MEDITATION

What are you afraid of?

Think of some actions and steps you can take to be courageous and do something in spite of your fears.

IT ALL STARTS WITH TAKING ONE SMALL STEP IN THE RIGHT DIRECTION.

*"Every individual suffers
from the fear of failure,
but you can change your destiny
only when you overcome it."*

~ ANUPAM KHER

Overcoming Failure

D id you know that the bigger you fail, the greater you succeed?

What? Yes, it's true: the greater you fail, the greater you succeed. Think about when you are learning a new job, trade, hobby, sport, or subject in school. Do you instantly succeed at everything? No. You have to learn and practice doing it to become better at it.

Practice makes perfect , right? … Well, that isn't always true. To overcome failure involves two key steps:

- **Never quit** — As long as you are willing to keep trying, you will be successful at some point as long as you integrate the next step.

- **Evaluate** — Whatever you do, always step back and evaluate what you did, what worked, what didn't work, and what can I do better?

We often need to undergo many failures and evaluation experiences before we become successful. The example I gave you earlier in the book about Thomas Edison (Day 3) is a great one to illustrate this.

Here are some other highly successful people we're all familiar with who had some spectacular failures:

- Oprah Winfrey, who became a household name because of her popular talk show was fired from many on-air jobs, with one former employer even going so far as to say she was too emotionally involved in the stories she reported.

- Steve Jobs, who is famous for his success with Apple computers, was fired by his own board of directors 10 years after he formed his company, but later came back and reinvented the company's image.

- Milton Hershey, one of the most well-known names in the candy industry, started three separate candy-related ventures that all failed before he had success with the Lancaster Caramel Company and eventually founded the Hershey Company.

- Stephen King, one of America's most prolific writers, was rejected 30 times before his first novel was published. King has now published 61 novels and 200 short stories.

MEDITATION

Whatever you do, step back and evaluate it. If it failed, figure out why and do better next time.

Ask yourself these questions:

- What did I do well?

- What can I improve?

- What will I do differently next time?

"It's fine to celebrate success
but it is more important
to heed the lessons of failure."

~ BILL GATES

53

"We all learn lessons in life.
Some stick, some don't.
I have always learned more
from rejection and failure
than from acceptance and success."

~ HENRY ROLLINS

Rejection

Being accepted and loved is important to our development, but we all experience rejection at some time in our lives. A big part of how rejection affects us depends on how we react, our age, and whom we have around us.

There are two types of rejection: overt and covert, or obvious and subtle. Some of the most damaging rejection can be done unintentionally. Frequently, the impact of rejection is felt emotionally without being understood intellectually; in other words, we sense it but can't explain it.

I am not going to get into all the ways rejection can occur, because I think it's more important right now to understand how to deal with rejection. Something I try to remember when I feel rejected, whether it was triggered by something said or done to me, is to not take it personally.

For example, let's say I am at work and I suggest eating at a particular place for lunch that I really enjoy, but everyone else shoots down my suggestion and says bad things about the place I like. They are not rejecting me; rather, they are rejecting the idea of eating at the place I suggested.

If we can start separating thoughts, actions, ideas, etc., from ourselves, we will find that we begin to look at things differently.

"I think that you have to believe
in your destiny;
that you will succeed;
you will meet a lot of rejection
and it is not always a straight path,
there will be detours —
so enjoy the view."

~ MICHAEL YORK

MEDITATION

Remind yourself that in most cases, people are rejecting an idea and not you. If they are rejecting you, then you do not need them in your life. If it is a family member or someone you have to be around for any period of time, then be careful how much time you spend with them so they don't bring you down.

You may want to take a long, hard look at what you can do to change your situation. Rejection is a very harmful thing when allowed to continue in your life.

The Rejection Syndrome by Charles R. Solomon explains in more detail how to understand rejection and what you can do about it. Even the Bible weighs in on rejection: "Your Creator thinks very highly of you and will never reject you because He formed you," Psalm, Chapter 139 speaks to this.

Remember, try not to take rejection personally.

*"Life is too short
to worry about anything.
You had better enjoy it
because the next day
promises nothing."*

~ ERIC DAVIS

DAY 16

Worry

Did you know that 50 percent of what you worry about will never happen?

A few other statistics that might interest you:

- 30 percent of the things you worry about are things that are over and done with — they can't be changed

- 12 percent of the things you worry about are needless unfounded worries about health

- 8 percent of what you worry about is real and legitimate

SO, WHY ARE WE WORRYING, WHEN WORRYING WON'T CHANGE A THING?

The definition of worry is to allow your mind to dwell on troubles or anything that makes you uneasy. It is a highly contagious disease that causes health problems for many people. Worry is self-perpetuating. It can become a habitual cycle, but the good news is the cycle can be broken.

There is a difference between worry and concern. Being concerned about something is when you see an issue and come up with a plan to either prepare for it or do something about it.

Fretting and worrying about something is unproductive and doesn't do you or anyone else any good.

Let's turn worrying thoughts around and dwell on things that will be productive and not destructive.

"I never worry about the problem.
I worry about the solution."

~ SHAQUILLE O'NEAL

MEDITATION

When you find yourself worrying, put the worry into one of the categories I described on page 59. If your worry falls into the real, legitimate worry category, then make a plan and be prepared to do something about it. If your worry falls into one of the other categories and you have no control over it, then it's time to move from worry to **being thankful.**

When worry hits, start thinking of all the things you are thankful for, and then thank God for them. Make this a habit and you will break the cycle of worry in your life.

A great reference book on worry is a book by James P. Gills, M.D. called *Rx for Worry: A Thankful Heart.*

"It does not mean you're broken to have depression and anxiety. I would encourage you to speak out.
Don't hold it inside.
Talk to friends.
Talk to parents.
If it's available, go to a therapist."

~ DAN REYNOLDS

Depression

How many times do we find ourselves feeling low and sorry for ourselves? When those feelings become more pronounced, they could be signs of depression. Depression can come on quickly. Knowing what triggers it and what helps bring you out of it can make all the difference in the world and make life a better place to be on a daily basis.

When you start to feel low, ask yourself these questions:

- Have I been eating healthy, nutritious food?
- Have I been getting enough sleep?
- Am I under stress?
- Am I comparing my life and circumstances to others in my life?
- How much time do I spend on social media?
- Have I been taking my medications prescribed by my doctor?
- When I look at a glass, do I see it as half-empty?

Remember what you learned yesterday about being thankful? A gratitude mindset is important for so many reasons. We can always find a silver lining to every dark cloud. I am someone who leans toward the positive, but it hasn't always been that way. You can train yourself to look for the good and have a positive outlook,which can change everything for the better.

There are so many things to be thankful for, but we many not always remember them, especially if we are feeling low.

If you struggle with depression,another important practice that can help you is to identify something you can look forward to, something to hope for. Each week, plan ahead to have something to look forward to. It might a movie night, date night, special dinner, activity with friends, crafting, or other things you enjoy.

"I found that with depression,
one of the most important things
you could realize is
that you're not alone."

~ DWAYNE JOHNSON

MEDITATION

Constantly remind yourself what you are thankful for and always have something to look forward to. To help you remember what you can be thankful for, make a list of all the good in your life. Some things you might include in the list are:

- Family

- Having good friends

- Being able to afford groceries

- Having a place to live

- Being employed

"Negative emotions like loneliness, envy, and guilt have an important role to play in a happy life; they're big, flashing signs that something needs to change."

~ GRETCHEN RUBIN

Loneliness

Who out there has not had the feeling of loneliness at some point in their lives? Ask yourself why you feel this way. When I have had to ask myself this question, the answer is often because I feel like no one understands what I am going through and no one cares.

When we have these feelings, we have to understand that they are not based on fact. Feelings are based on emotion and what our minds are telling us. Yes, we do feel this way, but it is possible to shift those feelings to bring yourself out of this place of feeling alone.

MINDSET ... HOPE ... GRATITUDE ... these all play a part in how we can transform feelings of loneliness.

I assure you that you are not alone. You can bring yourself from this place you feel like you cannot escape, if you really want to. So many others, including myself, have been where you are.

My next question is, who can you go to that would listen and be a sounding board for you? Sometimes, just talking out what you are feeling can really make a difference and help you work through these feelings.

Next, I want to tell you this: ***You are important and you are needed. You can make a difference in the world around you.***

YOU HAVE A PURPOSE!

As you look at your daily life and the people around you, ask yourself what can I do to make life better for someone else today? It could be a very small task, like buying a coffee for someone or helping someone with yard work. Find someone else to help.

I promise you, if you will do this and continue to do it on a daily basis, you will not feel alone anymore.

Let's take this one step further: look for a cause like the Red Cross, Salvation Army, or the Humane Society and volunteer to give back to your community. Start looking without and you will see a difference within.

MEDITATION

Look for the opportunities around you to be a blessing to others and become a part of something good that is bigger than just you. Make a list of some ways you can make this happen.

"Look for yourself,

and you will find in the long run only

hatred, loneliness, despair, rage,

ruin, and decay.

But look for Christ,

and you will find Him,

and with Him everything else thrown in."

~ C. S. LEWIS

"Unity is strength...
when there is teamwork
and collaboration,
wonderful things can be achieved."

~ MATTIE STEPANEK

Team

I want to expand on yesterday's reading because it goes hand in hand with what we are going to talk about today.

First, are you part of a community or team effort in some way? If not, then find a way to **DO IT!**

Google volunteer opportunities in your area. Search through Facebook groups for a topic of interest such as chess, cooking, crafting, etc., and join a group that interests you.

Teamwork makes the dream work. In my business, I teach an acronym for TEAM:

> **T**ogether
> **E**ach
> **A**chieves
> **M**ore

All big discoveries and major accomplishments in our world resulted from team effort. Many great leaders who have made an impact on our world with their discoveries and accomplishments had the help and teamwork of others.

Albert Einstein, the scientist who revolutionized the world with his theory of relativity, didn't work in a vacuum. Einstein once remarked, "Many times a day I realized how much my own outer and inner life is built upon the labors of my fellow men, both living and dead, and how earnestly I must exert myself in order to give in return as much as I have received."

On Day 4, I suggested you look up Walt Disney as an example of vision, but his life also demonstrates how it takes a team to transform a vision into reality. Walter Disney was the co-founder of Disney Productions. His brother, Roy, helped make their dream a reality. They didn't do it by themselves either. It took a massive amount of teamwork to bring about something so great.

"Teamwork can build friendships
that last a lifetime."

~NATALYA NEIDHART

MEDITATION

What do you want to be a part of?

What do you enjoy doing?

Find an organization that you can contribute to. You will feel a sense of significance when you are a part of something bigger than yourself.

Here are some examples that may offer opportunities to become part of a group: local service club like Sertoma or Kiwanis, volunteer at the local animal shelter, participate in church activities, or mentor a struggling student. There are endless possibilities, so choose what fits and will be rewarding for you.

"Depending on what they are, our habits will either make us or break us. We become what we repeatedly do."

~ SEAN COVEY

Habits

A big part of achieving your goal to make a change in your life is getting rid of bad habits and creating good ones. Today we will take a look at the four steps that lead to a changing or creating a habit.

Before you take the first step, you must become self-aware. Carl Jung said, "Until you make the unconscious conscious, it will direct your life, and you will call it fate."

We do a lot of things on autopilot without realizing it. The key to change is to start working on your systems of doing things. When you want to achieve long-term results in changing your habits, you are trying to change your identity and who you see yourself as. Make a decision today about the kind of person you desire and focus on the personality of who that is.

The four steps to forming a new habit or getting rid of a bad habit are:

- **Cue** — what your brain starts processing when it wants a particular reward.

- **Craving** — the motivation that comes with every habit.

- **Response** — the action or thought that is the habit.

- **Reward** — either the satisfaction or teaching and experience we get from the response.

If you want to develop a good habit, the cue needs to be obvious as well as the craving attractive. The craving needs to be something you want and are willing to do to make the creation of the new habit implementable. Have a system in place with intentional times and set guidelines to make the response easy and of course make the reward very satisfying.

"Old habits die hard,

and if you're not careful,

the person you used to be can

overtake the person you're trying to become.

~ LECRAE

MEDITATION

Think about what good habits you want to implement and start with one of them. Have a system in place based on the four steps outlined above to get this habit in place.

For example, a new habit I want to adopt is: I want to implement exercise.

I will take these four steps to create this new habit:

- **Cue** — when I wake up
- **Craving** — if there are certain shows that you enjoy watching, watch them when you are biking or running at the gym. Give yourself something to look forward to and only do this at the gym.
- **Response** — have your gym bag ready to go in the morning and your favorite show already uploaded.
- **Reward** — now you will have the reward of giving yourself that time to watch your show and are building a good habit of exercise.

Another idea to help you succeed is rewarding yourself after each week of exercise: a little shopping, eating out with friends, etc.

"Growth is the great separator between those who succeed and those who do not. When I see a person beginning to separate themselves from the pack, it's almost always due to personal growth."

~ JOHN C. MAXWELL

Intentional Personal Growth

D o you have a development plan in place for personal growth? Investing in yourself in different facets will help you become that person you want to be. If you do not set aside time to develop a plan, it most likely will never happen.

We need to be intentional. Here are the five practical steps to personal growth mentioned in John Maxwell's book,Developing the Leaders Around You.

FIVE STEPS FOR PERSONAL GROWTH

- Set aside time daily for growth.
- Quickly file what you learn.
- Quickly apply what you learn.
- Grow with someone.
- Plan your growth and follow it for a year.

If you take at least five days out of the week and spend fifteen to thirty minutes reading or listening to something that will help you grow in whatever areas you would like to learn, the personal growth within just one year will be noticeable. File those things you learn in a place you can refer back to easily in case you forget it and to just be able to go back and learn from it again or share it with others it could be useful to at a later time.

One of the most important things to remember is to put into practice what you learn as quickly as possible so it gets implemented into your life. Personal growth and learning is more fun when you have others to take it with you and plan what you are going to do on a daily basis and do it for a year.

Remember to enjoy the journey as you grow. The point of the journey is not in getting to the destination, but what you learn, who you meet, and what you become in the process.

MEDITATION

Find a book or books that explore the change you have chosen to make in your life and read for at least 10 minutes per day and implement what you learn as quickly as you can.. You can also find and listen to some relevant podcasts to reinforce your intention.

"Intelligent, successful, attractive people

can be intimidating.

They force us to hold a mirror

to ourselves;

we can be disappointed, jealous

or inspired toward personal growth."

~ IAN K. SMITH

"When self-doubt creeps in,
don't ignore it — address it.
Respond to harsh
self-criticism with
something more compassionate.
Talk to yourself like a
trusted friend and
refuse to believe your unrealistic,
negative inner monologue."

~ AMY MORIN

Self-Talk

I have woven self-talk into other meditations throughout this book. Why? Because it is crucial that you understand how much this affects your life.

You have the ability to change! It all starts with what you are telling yourself on a daily basis.

LISTEN TO YOUR INNER MENTOR INSTEAD OF YOUR INNER CRITIC

Today, I want us to pay attention to what we are telling ourselves and what we are listening to. Becoming self-aware is just part of the process we have been talking about.

Incorporate some intentional thoughts and consider what we are telling ourselves.

First, ask yourself what is a thought or action that you would like to change. For example, if people tell themselves that they are tired all the time, then they are going to be tired. A small action taken every day can create something new and start the ball rolling to turn it into something big.

When you catch yourself saying, "I am so tired," do the following:

- Stop yourself and count backwards: 5, 4, 3, 2, 1.

- Replace the negative sentence with: "I can feel the energy pumping!"

- Get on your feet and jump up and down like you mean it.

- After you have done all that, say: "Wow, I feel good!"

If you follow these guidelines, you will see they work.

"Relentless, repetitive self talk is what changes our self-image."

~ DENIS WAITLEY

MEDITATION

Pick out something to change about your self-talk today. Pay attention and take action.

Also, take 3x5-inch cards and write affirmations about what you are going to be and then post them all over your house.

Affirmations are the opposite of the negative things you are telling yourself.

An example would be: I am afraid others don't like me at work and that's why no one talks to me. An affirmation and your new plan to counteract that thought would be: I am very social at work and everyone wants to talk to me.

*"Nothing great
was ever achieved
without enthusiasm."*

~ RALPH WALDO EMERSON

Enthusiasm

Whenever someone asks, "How are you?" I always respond, "I am super great. If I were any better there would need to be two of me to contain it all."

You might say that you cannot be enthusiastic because of problems you're dealing with or how you are feeling.

I say, Baloney! Feelings come and go. You can change when you project differently.

To build on what we talked about yesterday on self-talk, what you confess determines what you possess!

Speak out loud what you want to see. If you don't like what you see, change what you are saying!

When you begin to *declare* you are enthusiastic, you will begin to *be* enthusiastic.

You have every reason to be enthusiastic and thankful because you have another day in this life to make a difference . You can change not only your life, but you can also make a difference in someone else's life. So, do it today!

Your belief will determine what you are receiving. It will shape your attitude and your outlook. A single positive thought repeated throughout the day can change your mindset.

If you don't believe me, try changing every negative thought you entertain to a positive one for thirty days. I'm positive you'll be surprised by what happens.

"Enthusiasm is the best protection

in any situation.

Wholeheartedness is contagious.

Give yourself, if you wish to get others."

~ DAVID SEABURY

MEDITATION

Every day when you wake up, declare: "I am so excited about what today is going to bring and my enthusiasm is going to be contagious."

When someone asks how you are, you are going to respond with, "I feel so good that I don't know if I can contain it!" You don't have to say those exact words, obviously you can customize it so it works for you.

I also want you to write down these statements on a 3x5-inch card and say them to yourself throughout the day.

You may not believe it at first, but as you continue to practice these principles, you will begin to not only believe it but feel it.

"Our bodies change our minds and our minds can change our behavior and our behavior can change our outcomes."

~ AMY CUDDY

DAY 24

Superhero Pose

You may be wondering, what in the world is this? The Superhero Pose is when you stand tall with your legs spread apart, arms on your hips, elbows bent, chest puffed out, and head facing in an upward position like you are getting ready to face your inferior opponent. The pose is also referred to as the power pose.

Harvard social scientists affirm that this powerful posture increases testosterone (dominance hormone) about 20 percent, while dropping cortisol (stress hormone) 25 percent. Other research indicates that power posing for two minutes can change your physiology.

POWER POSING CAN TRANSFORM YOU

When you do this pose, you will feel more confident, comfortable, and enthusiastic. Using the power pose daily can change the way you think and talk during events, phone calls, interviews, etc.

Doing this will help you to exude confidence you never knew you had.

If you don't believe me, I challenge you to try it. Tell me how you feel after just a week.

Successful people often exude confidence —

it's obvious that they believe in themselves

and what they're doing.

It isn't their success

that makes them confident, however.

The confidence was there first.

~ TRAVIS BRADBERRY

MEDITATION

Do you want to feel like a superhero?
Try out your power pose!
Do your power pose at least
once a day and before every
important event or phone call.

"We can change the world if we change ourselves. We just need to get hold of the old patterns of thinking and dealing with things and start listening to our inner voices and trusting our own superpowers."

~ NINA HAGEN

"*Do or do not.*

There is no try."

~ YODA, *THE EMPIRE STRIKES BACK*

Trying

What does "try" actually mean? According to the dictionary, it is a verb that means to make an attempt or effort to do something.

Let's take that one step further and also define attempt: it means to make an effort to achieve or complete.

When you think about *trying* to do something, does that produce feelings of doubt or falling short of doing what you are attempting?

I would like to do an experiment with you right now. Place a pencil or pen on top of the nearest table. I want you to "try" to pick it up.

Understand, I did not say, "Pick it up." I said to "try" to pick it up. Think about this for a minute.

When you *try* to do something, are you actually doing it? No, you are *attempting* to do it. I would like you to change your trying to actually doing.

Whatever goals or projects you have before you that you are *trying* to do, **stop trying!** Instead, I want you to say:

"I will finish my projects. I am on my way to accomplishing my goals."

Now you are **doing!**

Just like the NIKE slogan I love … Just Do It!™™

"Start by doing what's necessary;
then do what's possible;
and suddenly you are doing the impossible."

~FRANCIS OF ASSISI

MEDITATION

Figure out what you need to do to accomplish your goals and finish your projects. Once you've determined this, work toward doing it.

Do not fall into the trap of saying you are "trying" to do something —because chances are, you will never get it done!

"Life...

It tends to respond to our outlook,

to shape itself to meet our expectations."

~ RICHARD M. DEVOS

Expectation

Another word I use for expectation is hope. I have found that life is so much better on a daily basis when you have something to hope for. Have a new expectation every single day.

It's been said that you experience what you expect. Tell yourself daily, "Good things are happening to me."

We all have had those times when we expected something and it didn't come to pass and then we were greatly disappointed. But life always has disappointments. It is more about what you do with the disappointments than the disappointments themselves. When we have those let-downs, we need to look for the opportunity to use those lemons to make lemonade.

What might that look like? Here's an example:

I had been looking forward to attending a friend's wedding and I was really excited to spend some time with everyone and catch up. I ended up getting sick and couldn't go.

I could let this disappointment cause me to mope around and feel sorry for myself all day. Or, I could look at this as an opportunity. I could use this time to catch up on some reading or binge watch a series I've wanted to see.

The moral of this story: look for and enjoy the best no matter what happens.

I wake up every morning with the expectation that something good is going to happen today. I go to my mailbox with the expectation that I will find something good in there. Some days I find something good, and some days I don't. My attitude is, "There's always tomorrow, and I might find something good then."

If you are having a hard time with expectation and looking for the good things that are happening, then we need to change that. The first thing I would like you to do is pick one thing you are expecting to be good in the next week. If you are a believer in God, then I have a couple of other thoughts and actions for you:

PUSH

Pray
Until
Something
Happens

Expectation — Ask in faith, write it down, and thank God for what you are expecting. Confess what you want to possess and believe that you can receive it.

MEDITATION

Have an expectation every day that something good is going to happen.

Write these down and reflect on these expectations and what actually happened when the day is done.

"High expectations
are the key to everything."

~SAM WALTON

*"You are bigger
than your self-doubt.
Remind yourself of that
each and every day."*

~ CAROLINE GHOSN

Doubt

How often do feelings of self-doubt haunt your mind? Thoughts like,this is too big for me, I am not ready for this, I am not good enough, or I don't deserve this. Or do you hear an inner voice saying, "not me" or "never could be me." That is the voice of self-doubt, or some might call it the inner critic. **STOP!**

It's important to realize that we all have these feelings from time to time, but we need to change our focus and our thoughts about who we are and what we are capable of.

Your self-doubt is not only costing you, but all those people that you could be affecting in a positive way. We need to learn to live with this inner voice of doubt, but we don't have to be ruled by it. Instead, learn to be moved by it and work through the doubts that you have and turn them around for your success.

When you begin to doubt yourself, ask why. Gather the appropriate information on how to do or what you need to do that can move you forward away from what you are doubting about yourself. Look for solutionsto the problems you are facing. Remember, the faster you fail as you move forward, the faster you will succeed. No one is just successful all of a sudden. It takes time to fail and learn from your mistakes to make a go of it and be successful.

When you study some of the most successful people in history, you will find out that they were not always successful. They too had many failures.

"The Savior isn't our last chance; He is our only chance. Our only chance to overcome self-doubt and catch a vision of who we may become. Our only chance to repent and have our sins washed clean."

~SHERI L. DEW

MEDITATION

Believe in yourself and find solutions to the things you have been waiting to do because of your self-doubt. Move forward and start acting upon where you want to be and what you want to accomplish.

When that voice of self-doubt tries to overtake you, overcome that voice with a plan to move forward and in confidence state, "I am successful in everything I do and will learn more and continue to propel myself forward by doing rather than wishing."

A wish is just a wish until you act upon it.

"Hate is self-destructive. If you hate somebody, you're not hurting the person you hate. You're hurting yourself. And that's a healing. Actually, it's a real healing, forgiveness."

~ LOUIS ZAMPERINI

Hurt & Forgiveness

We all get our feelings hurt from time to time. It is an unavoidable truth. I have found that learning to work through the hurt and forgiveness will free you from the pain and long-term negative effects.

The greatest hurt is when it comes from someone close to you and you have to be around that person on a daily basis. Sometimes the offender does not even know that they have hurt you. In this situation, I have used one of these two methods:

My first method is to approach my offender and say something along the lines of, "Do you remember when you said this (or did this)? I was really hurt by it and I felt _____ (explain what you felt when it occurred)."

I go on to say that I may have taken what was said or done in the wrong way or misinterpreted it, but that it really hurt me. Allow them the time to speak on their behalf and then talk about why it hurt and work through the forgiveness process.

If the offender just shrugs off the offense, it is important to remember that holding onto that hurt is giving them a permanent place to hurt you.

What I have done when someone has hurt me, and they don't feel they did anything wrong, is to continually confess that I have forgiven them and that they have no hold on me. Depending on how deep the hurt and how often you have been hurt by this person, this action may have to be repeated daily — possibly many times a day — for months.

It took me a whole year of doing this to finally forgive the person who had deeply hurt me, but now I do not have that stabbing pain of hurt when I think of them or see them.

If you believe in God, then take this to the Lord in prayer daily and He will help you forgive. You must make the choice to forgive the offense and the offender, even before you feel like you can. It's a choice that will set you free from whatever or whoever has hurt you. Cut the ties.

The second way of handling the hurt or offense is to go through the process of forgiveness that I just spoke of without going to the offender. Many times, you will know whether saying something to the offender will do any good. If possible, choose who you are with wisely. If you are able to distance yourself from the offender, then do it. Long-term mental and physical damage can occur if this situation is left unchecked.

MEDITATION

Make a list of people who have hurt you. When the list is complete, begin the process of forgiveness.

"*Holding on to anger, resentment and hurt only gives you tense muscles, a headache and a sore jaw from clenching your teeth. Forgiveness gives you back the laughter and the lightness in your life.*"

~ JOAN LUNDEN

"Ability is what you're capable of doing. Motivation determines what you do. Attitude determines how well you do it."

~LOU HOLTZ

Attitude

Attitude determines your altitude. If there is one thing you can control, it is your attitude. You may not be able to control others or what happens around you but you sure can control what happens in you.

Did you know that your attitude towards others determines their attitude towards you? Do a little experiment. When you go to the store, I want you to smile and say hello enthusiastically to people as they go by and see what their reactions are. After you do this with a handful of people, put your meanest face on and start grumbling and complaining and make some sort of complaint to them. I want you to see how people respond.

Generally, people will mirror what they see. They will reflect your attitude. Attitudes are contagious.

According to Stanford Research Institute, your success in life is greater with a positive mental attitude. Positive thoughts can actually create real value in your life and can help you build real skills that will benefit you for a lifetime.

Your mind is like a garden; put good things in and you will reap the benefits. On the flip side, when you put garbage in, garbage will come out. It is so important to read positive books, listen to positive content, and associate with positive people.

You can learn to be a thermostat rather than a thermometer. The thermometer goes up and down according to the situation. A thermostat controls and regulates!

If there is one thing you can do that will alter your life on a daily basis, that would be to feed your mind positive content every day. John Maxwell has a lot of books and video content on this subject. Read or listen to something positive for even five to ten minutes and then pick out one thought to think on for the day. Send it to yourself in an email or text or write it down on a piece of paper or 3x5-inch card to carry with you. Reiterate this thought to yourself throughout the day. You will find that this will begin to change your thinking.

Remember the methods we talked about earlier in the book? Use the five-second rule or the cancel-cancel method when negative thoughts come and replace them with positive ones. It is about reprogramming the mind.

MEDITATION

Find one positive thing to focus on every day.

Greet the day and others with a positive attitude.

Keep your attitude hot and even those that have a negative attitude around you will eventually get a little bit of that fire burning.

"It is our attitude at the beginning of a difficult task which, more than anything else, will affect its successful outcome."

~ WILLIAM JAMES

"Failing doesn't have to mean not succeeding. It can be, 'Hey we tried that. We can go forward, smarter."

~ ASTRO TELLER

Failing Forward

Fear of failure is at the top of the list of reasons why people do not move forward. Fear of failure prevents people from becoming all that they could be and prevents them from doing all they could do.

FACT:

EVERYONE IS GOING TO FAIL AT SOME POINT.

FACT:

NOT EVERYONE IS GOING TO PROFIT FROM HIS OR HER FAILURE.

Failure is far more common that success, but failure can be used to propel you forward into success. I am going to share with you just a few of the ideas that John Maxwell writes about in his book, *How to Fail Forward*. These ideas have made a significant difference in my life. If you have never read this book, it's a great idea to read it soon.

Attitude and mindset need to be focused on what can result from and be learned from the failure. Doing this will mean you can be that much better next time.

My biggest take-away from reading *How to Fail Forward* is that I need to look at all failure in a positive way. Looking at negative experiences as a learning process allows you to grow in the midst despite the failure.

Use your failures to propel you forward and don't ever give up.

"A little more persistence,
a little more effort,
and what seemed hopeless failure
may turn to glorious success."

~ ELBERT HUBBARD

MEDITATION

Remember that every failure can be a learning experience and every mistake gets you that much closer to your goals.

Re-evaluate what you are doing, figure out what went wrong and then make the necessary changes to make your next attempt a success.

*"Your self-worth
has nothing to do with
your craft or calling,
and everything to do with
how you treat yourself.*

~ KRIS CARR

Self-Worth

Who determines your self-worth? According to the dictionary, worth is defined as the value equivalent to that of someone or something under consideration; the level at which someone or something deserves to be valued or rated.

No one can determine your value, for you are priceless. Why do I say that? You have been created with a purpose in mind and there is no one else exactly like you. Understand, we all have our faults and we are not perfect, but no one can be that difference maker in the world around you but YOU.

You are not serving anyone by playing it small and not living up to the potential that you can be. You have a lot to offer and people are out there waiting for you to come into their world.

Don't let the IF part of LIFE take its place anymore. "If only," I hear it said. Let's change that to "next time" and use every experience as opportunity for growth. You are worth the investment to become a better you.

MEDITATION

Think about the value you create, not only in yourself, but also in those lives that you are able to invest in.

Take the time every day to invest in yourself, and look for the opportunities to invest in others to show them what you've learned. You will feel no greater sense of self-worth than when you are investing in others like you invest in yourself.

"Hateful words stand no chance against self-worth and a little of humor."

~ ISKRA LAWRENCE

Conclusion

One day at a time and one step at a time, you will move forward to what you have been seeing in yourself but were unsure about how to achieve.

If you want the principles and changes I've talked about in this book to become a part of your life forever, I suggest you make it a habit to reread this book every month for the next three months.

If you want to grow faster and dive deeper into the information I've presented, start a group with a handful of people to go through the book together. Why? When you bring together a few different people to go over the same material, each person comes with a different perspective, opinion, and view. It is always more fun to grow together.

About the Author

Marsha Jackson is a licensed pastor and co-owner with her husband of a successful wellness consulting business, R&M Wellness. She has counseled and taught thousands of people on relationships, marriage, business practices, women, leadership, and other life and work topics.

The principles in *Life Without Limits* are the ones Marsha has taught over and over again to help people make positive changes. She wanted to put these principles in a simple, easy-to-read book format so everyone might have access to them and begin applying them immediately. Most importantly, she wanted people to be able to learn and practice these principles without investing hours in reading and implementing them.

"Now and Later" is Marsha's motto for her proven approach to transformation. She offers short daily readings and meditations to give readers something to quickly grasp and act on now while setting a solid foundation for change and growth later.

Marsha and her husband have four children and live in upstate New York.

To book Marsha for events
or to discuss questions about this book,
please email her directly *at:*

marsha@mkjbooks.com

visit the author's website:

LifeWithoutLimitsBook.com

READ

the subject matter for the day

REFLECT

on what you have just read

and how it applies to you

RESET

your mind to begin

the new thought processes

REDO

and make the necessary changes

to complete the action steps

ENJOY THE NEW YOU!

Made in the USA
Monee, IL
22 June 2021